Illustrated by
Kathy Gilchrist

# Where is Thumbkin?

**Color the twins.**
**Play them on your piano.**

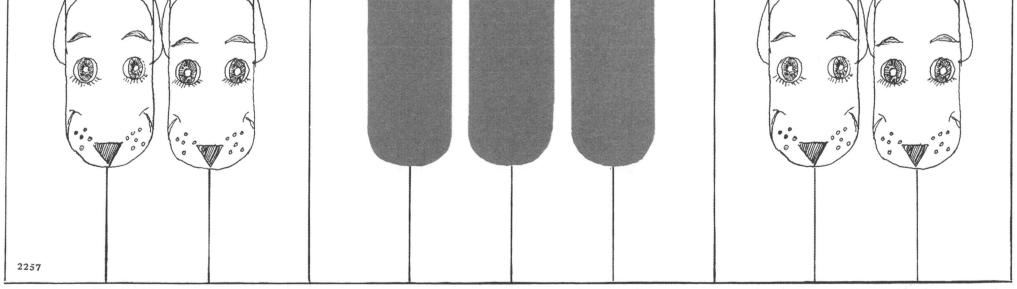

# Elephants

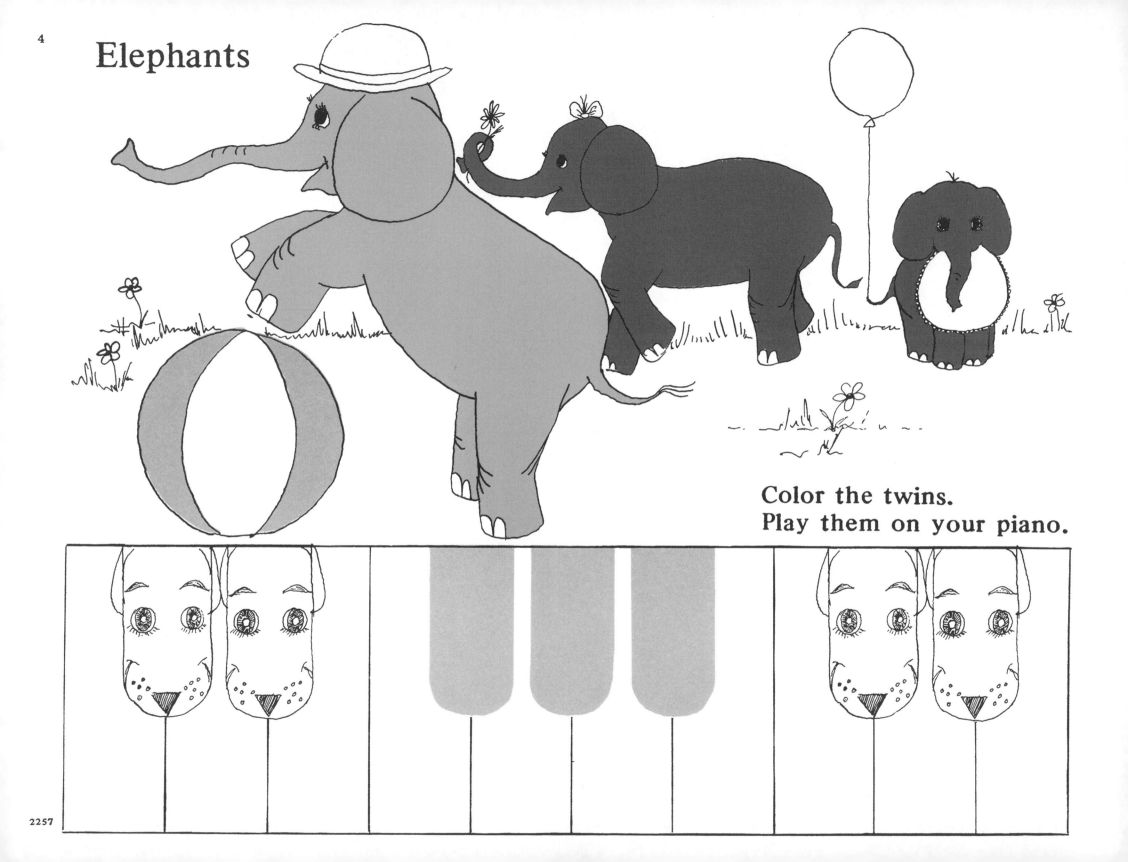

Color the twins.
Play them on your piano.

## Color the triplets.
## Play them up high on your piano.

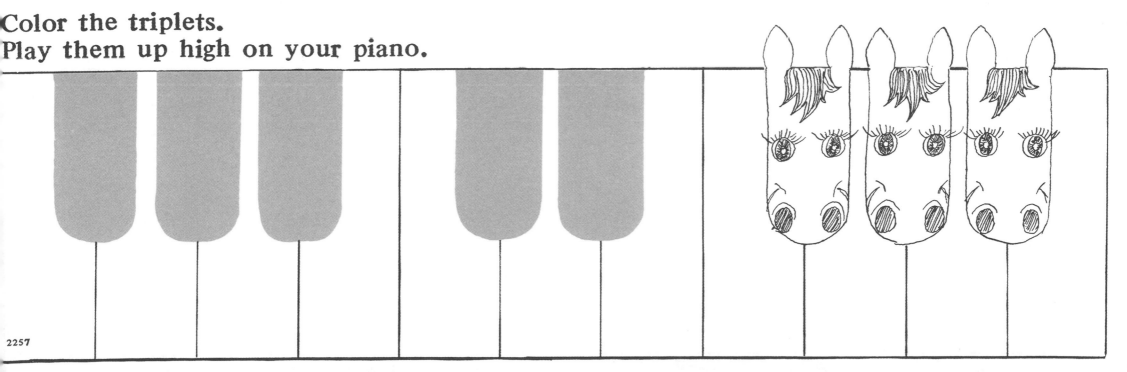

# Scuba

Color the triplets.
Play them down low on the piano.

# Farmer in the Dell

2257

# Jack and Jill

Jack and Jill went up the hill to fetch a pail of wa - ter.

Jack fell down and broke his crown and Jill came tumb-ling af - ter.

# Plip—Plop

Rain, rain, go a - way! Come a - gain some oth - er day.

# Mister Giraffe

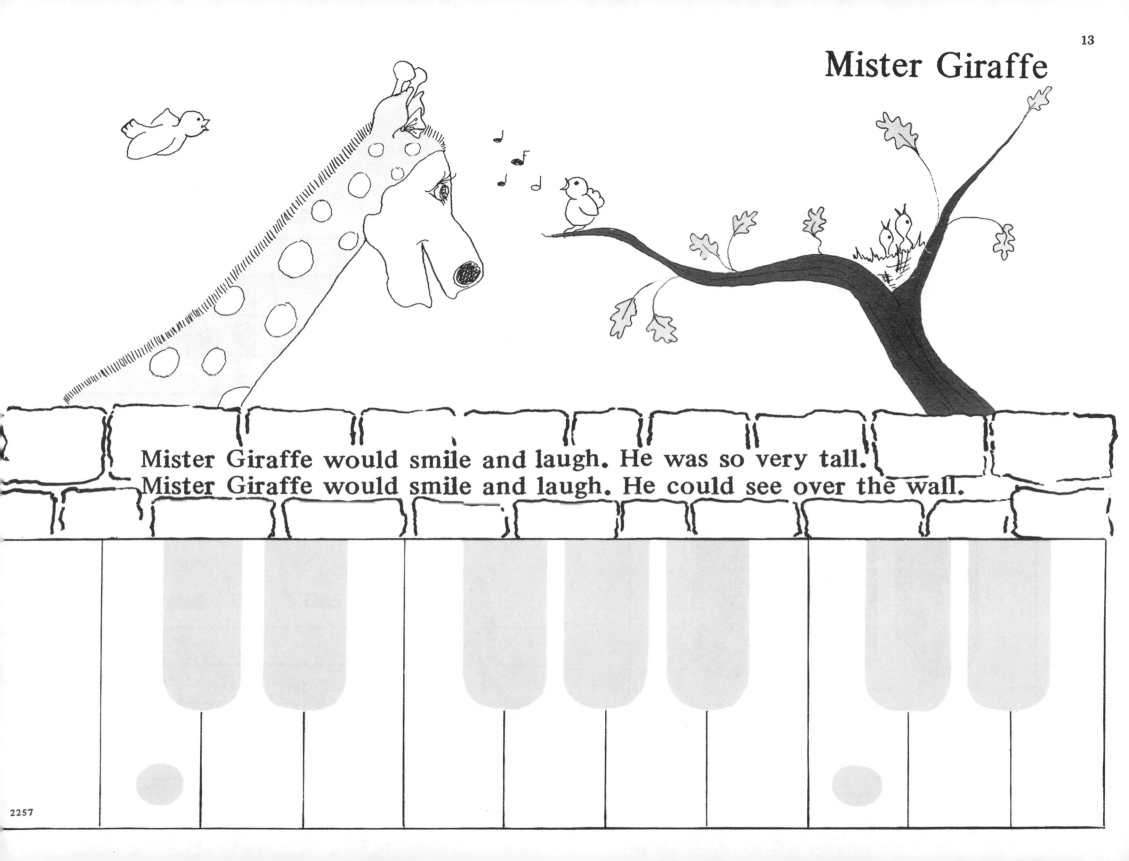

Mister Giraffe would smile and laugh. He was so very tall.
Mister Giraffe would smile and laugh. He could see over the wall.

2257

# Listening Game

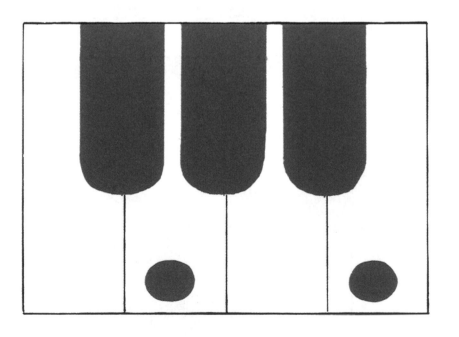

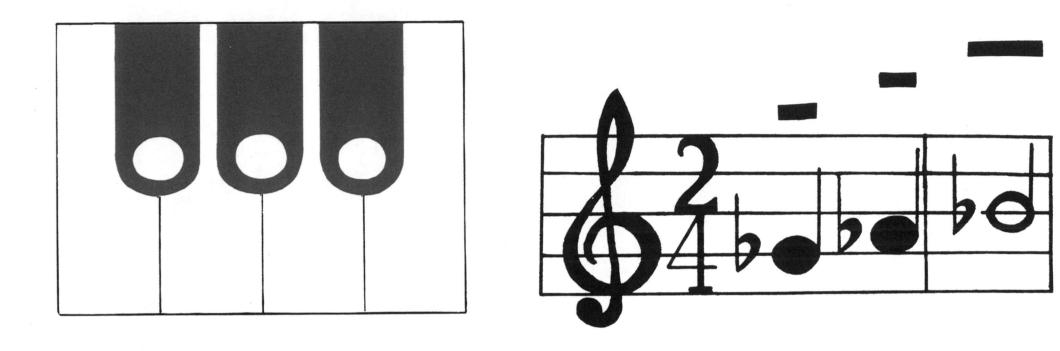

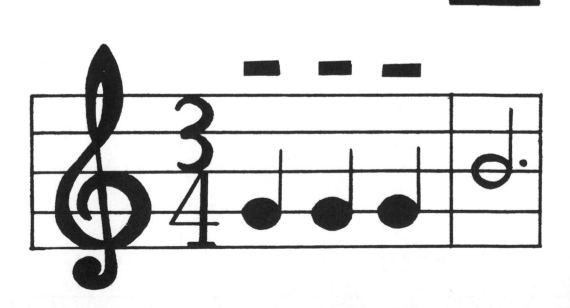

# Indian Dance

# Three Blind Mice

# Play—A—Story

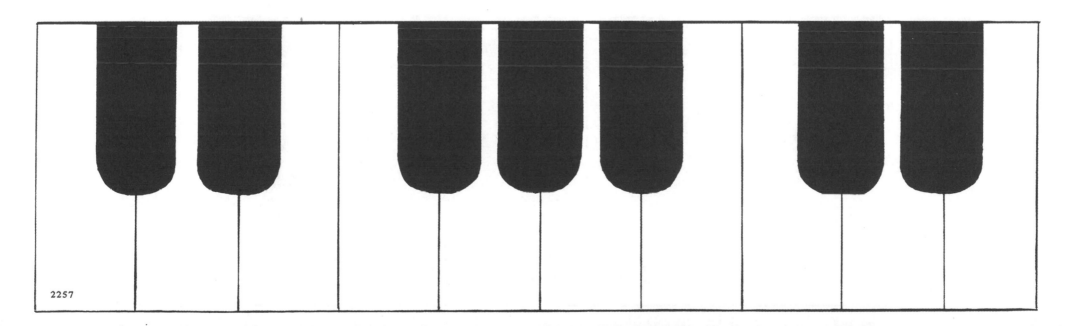

# Shh - - - Listen

Shh - Listen!
Somebody do something!
Can't you hear? He is
There in the corner so
Terribly near!

Shh - Listen!
Who is that hiding? What
Crawly creature? His
Bright shining eyes are a -
Glow in the dark!

Shh - Listen!
Click on the light. What an
Awful fright! Why it's
Only my dog busy
Scratching his ear!
Whew!

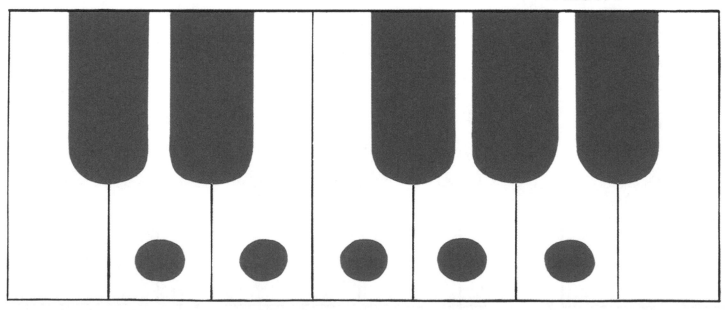

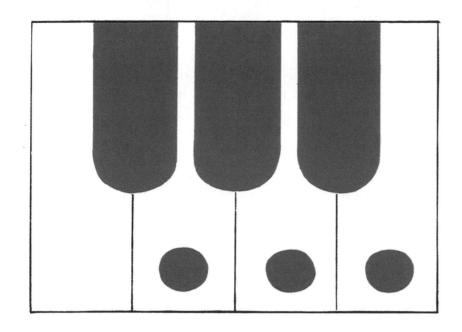

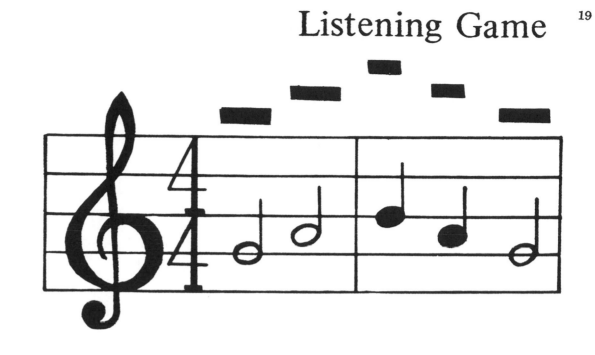

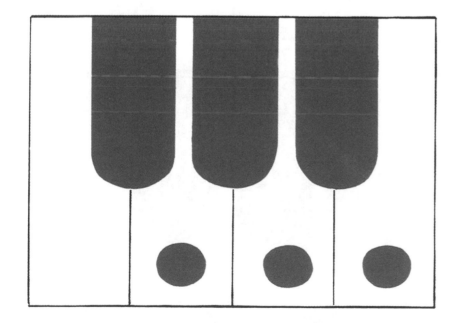

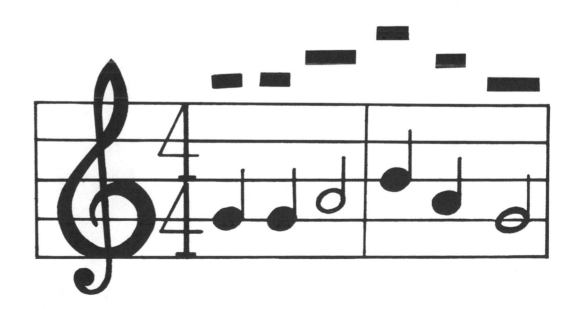

# Spooky Voices

Whooo.........?

# Hickory Dickory Dock

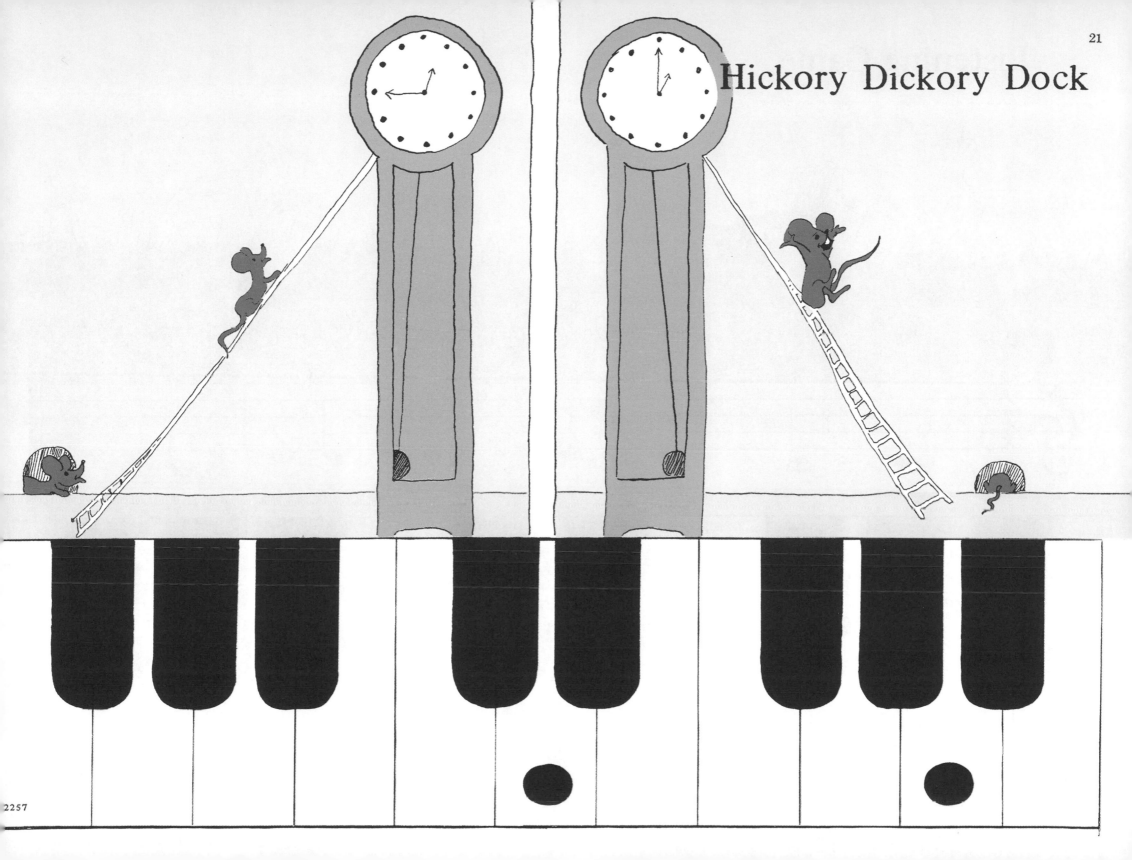

# Listening Game

# Listening Game

# Up the Hill

Step     up,     step     up.     Step     up     the     hill.

2257

# Down the Hill

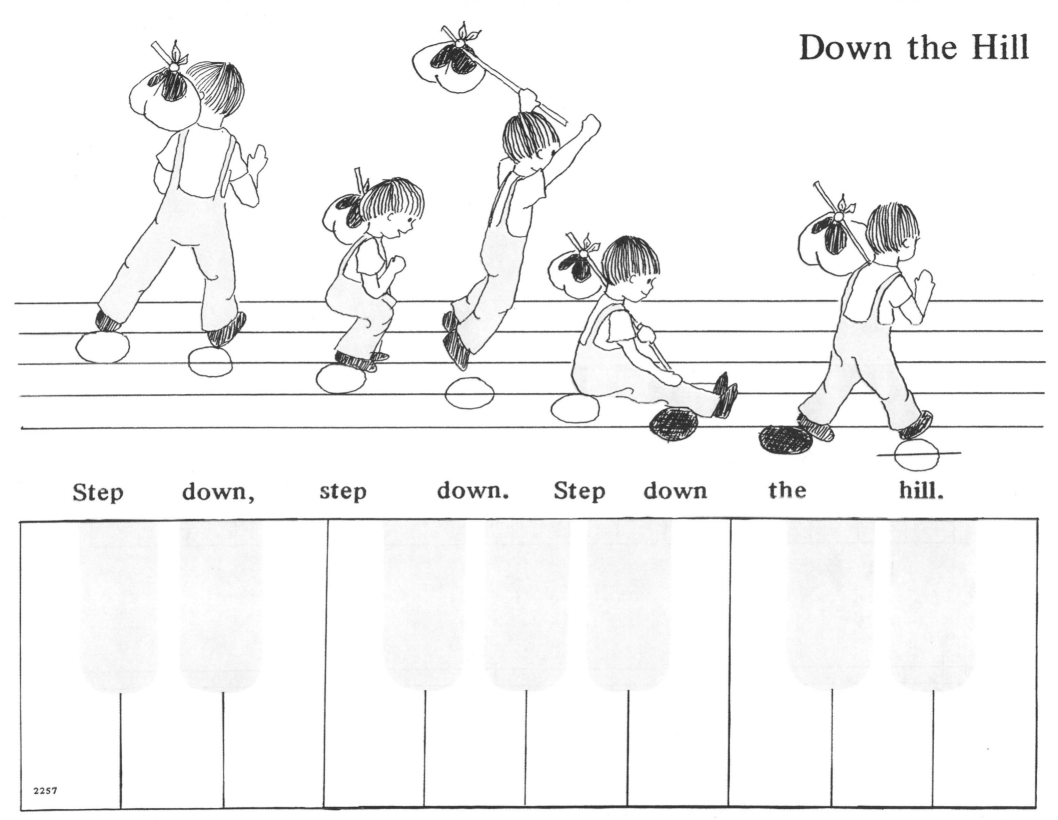

Step    down,    step    down.    Step    down    the    hill.

2257

# My Pony

My po-ny's name is Spor-ty Spot. Tip, tip, Tip- i - yea.
He runs and trots and nev-er stops. Tip, tip, Tip- i - yea.

# Thanksgiving Song

A  tur-key ran a - way  be-fore Thanks-giv-ing  day.  Said

A pumpkin ran away
before Thanksgiving day.
Said he, "They'll make a
pie out of me if
I should stay!"

A cranberry ran away
before Thanksgiving day.
Said he, "They'll make a
sauce out of me if
I should stay!"

he, "They'll make a roast out of me if I should stay!"

# Tune—Up (Left Hand)

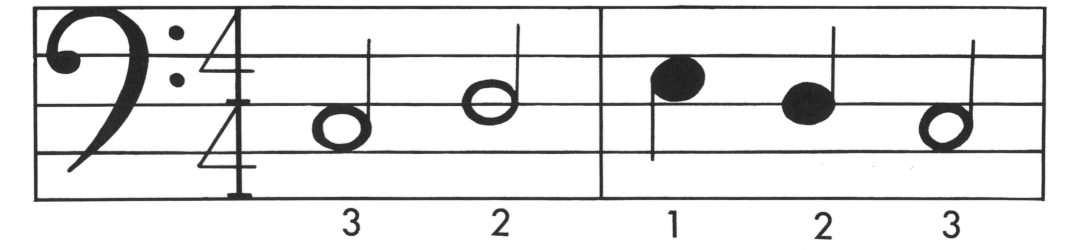

# Tune—Up (Right Hand)

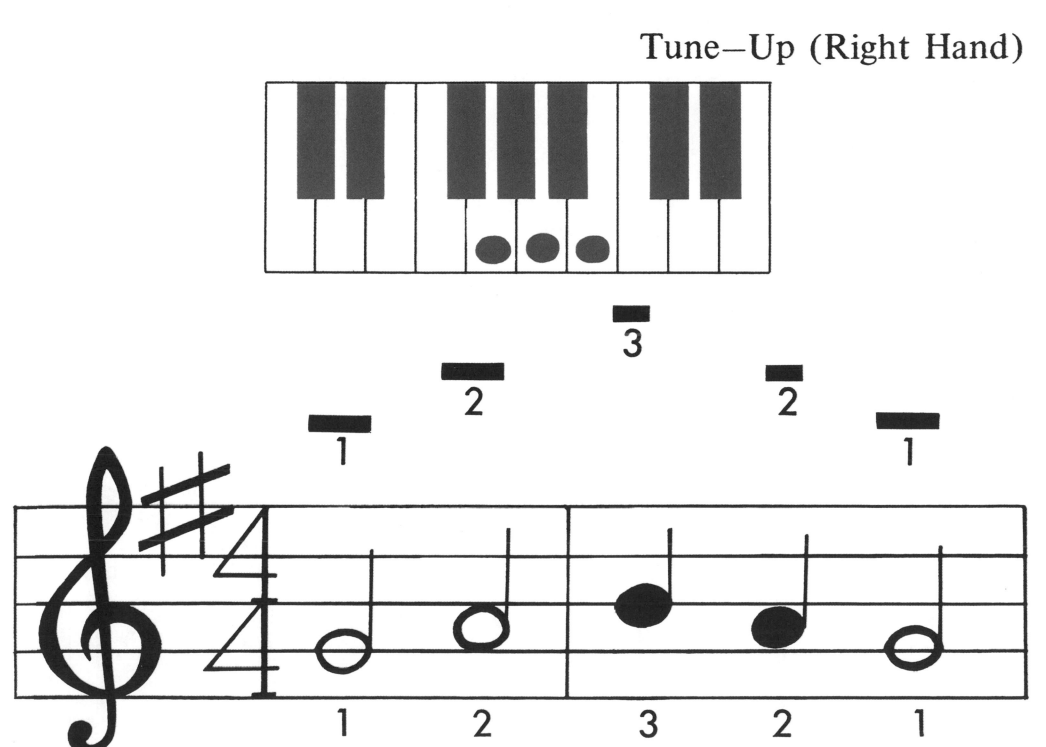

# A–Hunting We Will Go

Oh a - hunt-ing we will go. A - hunt-ing we will go. We'll

catch a lit -tle fox and put him in a box ,and then we'll let him go.

Oh a - hunt-ing we will go. A - hunt-ing we will go. We'll

catch a lit-tle fox and put him in a box, and then we'll let him go.

# Peter, Peter, Pumpkin Eater

**Peter, Peter Pumpkin eater.**
**Had a wife and couldn't keep her.**

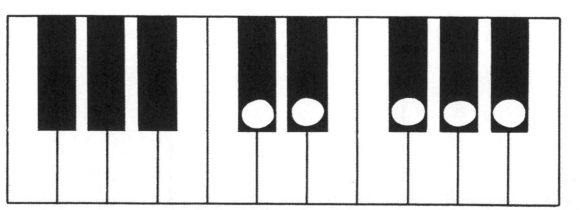

Put her in a pumpkin shell          and there he kept her very well!

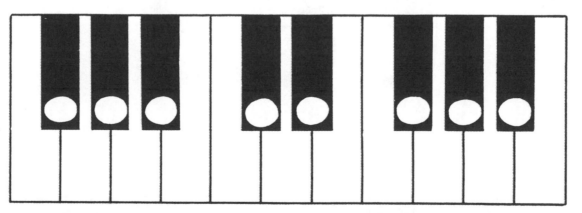

# Hot Cross Buns

Hot    cross    buns.    Hot    cross    buns.

# Question and Answer

Question  Answer

How are you?

Question  Answer

How are you?

Question  Answer

Who has a pup-py?

# Snowflakes

Snowflakes danc-ing    on    the    ground. Snowflakes, snowflakes all  a - round.
Soft- ly,   gent-ly    in    the    air.   Snowflakes, snowflakes ev'-ry - where.

# Mister Snowman

Roll-ing up and down and up the snow-man grows so fat.
Eyes and nose and smil - ing mouth and now a fun - ny hat.

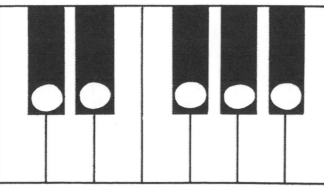

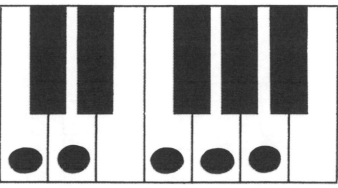

# Question and Answer

**Question**       Answer

**Question**       Answer

# Jingle Bells

Jin- gle bells, Jin- gle bells, Jin- gle all the way. Oh what fun it

1st ending

2nd ending

is to ride in a one horse o - pen sleigh, one horse o - pen sleigh.

# Frère Jacques

Frè- re  Ja-cques,  Frè- re  Ja-cques, Dor- mez vous? Dor- mez vous?

Son-nez les ma-ti-nes,   Son-nez les ma-ti-nes, Ding, ding, dong. Ding, ding, dong.

# Question and Answer

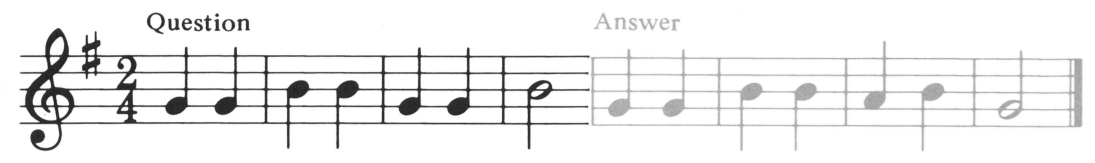

**Question**      Answer

**Question**      Answer

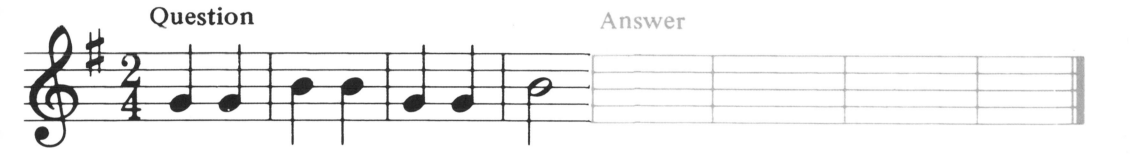

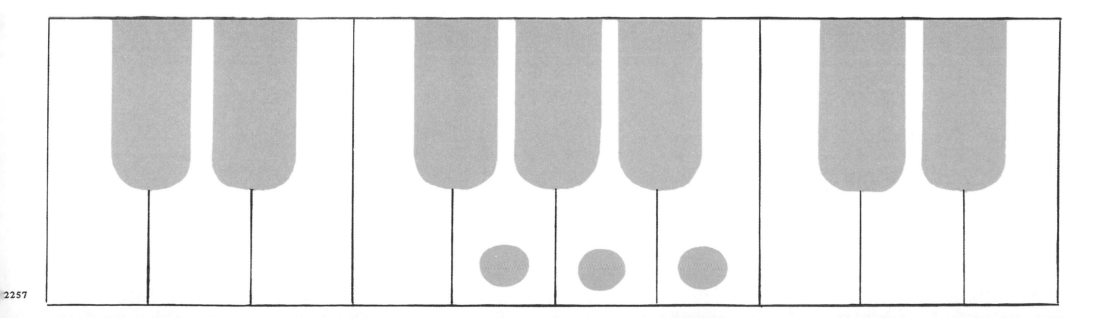

# Old King Cole

Old King Cole was a merry old soul and a merry old soul was he! He

called for his pipe, and he called for his bowl, and he called for his fiddlers three.
" " " " " " " " " " " " " " " " drummers three.
" " " " " " " " " " " " " " " " buglers three.

Dance to the fiddlers,  Dance to the fiddlers,  Dance to the fiddlers  three.
" " " drummers,  " " " drummers,  " " " drummers  three.
" " " buglers,  " " " buglers,  " " " buglers  three.

# Farmer in the Dell

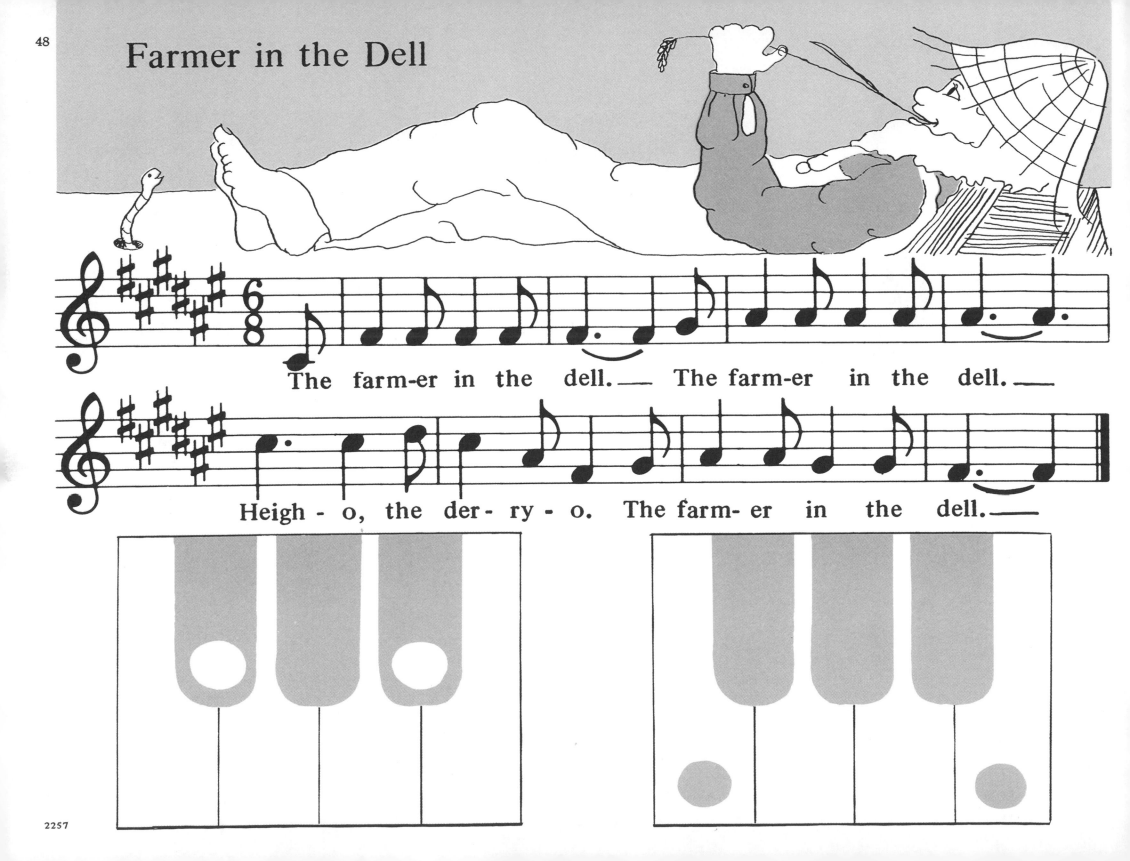

The farm-er in the dell. — The farm-er in the dell. —

Heigh - o, the der - ry - o. The farm-er in the dell. —